FOR A REASON

Keys from God to help you through
unexpected crises

Matthew Brown

CONTENTS

INTRODUCTION

One day after prayer I felt God saying write down what you have learned. I went through a period in my life in which my world was unexpectedly turned upside down. Many of the things I had depended on like key relationships, my calling, the institution I was a part of and my own relationship with God were all suddenly called into question. I was facing a loss that I thought I never would have to endure. I don't know whether you have some lines that you feel God is not to cross, for instance; "It's all fine as long as I don't lose my Job", "I can cope as long as I have my family" "As long as my husband doesn't leave" "It will be ok as long as the kids are happy". Then one day you find that red line is passed, and you are left wondering how to get through. Maybe everything that you once believed is now being questioned and you are unsure how to move forward.

There is a story in Exodus 17 where the Israelites have escaped slavery and Egypt only to find themselves in a strange land being attacked by an army of Amalekites. The Israelites were in a new unknown land with little organisation or help. The Amalekites were in a land they knew and were ordered and ready! The solution: Moses held his staff up to God over the battle and as long as he kept his hand raised the Israelites won the battle. God fought the battle for them, and ultimately they overcame.

I found myself in an unknown land, a new situation with little support around me to face the situation that I encountered, much like the Moses and his people in the previous paragraph. I did not know where to turn but I knew God and so I tried my best to turn to Him! At times I felt he had deserted me and thought that He was the one who had put me in this situation. In the end, however, I learned that He was my constant support at my side pulling me through it all. I had been called by God to Rio de Janeiro for 15 years and we finally arrived as a family. It was the promised land and in arriving it felt like so many of the promises we had waited for were finally being fulfilled. I did not have any idea of what was around the corner. I don't need to go into the details but after a period of difficulties I found myself facing the loss of my marriage, ministry and possibly my place in the city that I had felt called to for so long. I did, in the end, lose my marriage and resign from ministry feeling that, at that point, it was not right to continue. However, a new door opened to teach in a Christian international school at which my children were students and so we were able to continue to live and work in Rio. It was a time where the promises God had made, and the dreams of my heart, seemed to fall apart at my feet.

I write because I have a hunch that many people out there may have also faced the loss of what they felt God had called them to, or seen their dreams collapse to what seems to be nothing. I decided to write about the things that sustained me through this time and re-established my trust in God. There were times where I nearly gave up and walked away but I now see that it was "For a Reason!" Perhaps that reason is to help others through situation of darkness or heartbreak and encourage them to hold on to God! He is for you, and though you might not see it, what you go through now will in the end be "For a reason"!

NEVER ALONE

One of the biggest problems of our time is loneliness. We are connected in every way we could wish to be. We have the internet, social media, more platforms than have ever existed to keep in touch and yet people still feel the deep ache of loneliness. Why is this? I wonder whether our relationships are more numerous but of less depth than they have been. It is easy to press a thumbs up or give a quick congratulations for a birthday: it no longer takes an effort. Relationships really require effort. Society now gives quick responses and quick solutions for everything. Maybe we want quick relationships in the same way, but these are just not fulfilling because we never really get to know people.

It is also possible to have people around us and be in contact but still feel very alone. I went through this experience. Some circumstances we go through can be extremely isolating. There are situations which we alone face and unless you go through that experience you find that others can't fully comprehend. These kinds of situations can involve unexpected trauma, loss through death or the end of a relationship, abuse, loss of a career, moving to a new country, sickness and I am sure others. When we go through these things, more than ever, we need to know we are not alone! Maybe right now you are reading this and feeling alone or abandoned. Please don't give up! You are not alone. Your life has purpose and meaning and though you might not see it right now you would leave a hole in other people's lives that no one else could replace! I understand what it is like to wake and think "What's the point" and to pull the cover over your head again. I have curled up in a corner and cried because I did not know where to turn. I have had the thoughts that maybe it would just be best if I was no longer here. Those things are very real and painful. But hold on! This is a season, a difficult time, it might be short, it might be long, but another season will come. Spring will come the buds will come up, the birds will start to sing, and the days will get brighter. Go and find someone you trust to speak to and don't suffer in silence. If there is no one then there are many emergency lines out there to call. Make contact and don't quit!

I had a friend who would keep in touch with me and though he was in another country his support was a lifeline to me, via WhatsApp. He regularly reminded me of this verse: *"I will never leave you nor forsake you." (Joshua 1:5, Hebrews 13:5 NIV).* At times it did not feel true but that did not mean it was not true. To hear that from someone who cared made a huge difference to me. It might not feel like it but it is true, God is a loving Dad who cares desperately about all of His children. He wants us to understand that we are never left alone he is always alongside us through the hardest of days!

I really like the film Castaway and it gives an interesting picture of what it would really be like to be isolated. In the film Chuck, played by Tom Hanks, works for FedEx and is on a plane that crashes in the middle of the ocean. He is washed up on a deserted Island and has to make it on his own. He eventually makes it off the island and is rescued 4 years after his initial disappearance. There is a scene at the end of the movie in which he is talking to one of his colleagues and reflecting on what happened. During this scene he reflected on a moment he tried to commit suicide and it went wrong. He comments "I couldn't even kill myself the way I wanted. I had power over nothing. That's when this feeling came over me like a warm blanket that I somehow had to stay alive, that I had to keep breathing even though I had no reason to hope". He goes on to say "'one day the tide came in and it brought me a sail and now here I am" and then finally "and now I know what I have to do: got to keep breathing because tomorrow the sun will rise and who knows what the tide could bring?" To be isolated for four years would feel pretty hopeless but as he comments at the end, each day the sun does rise and the tide comes in and we never know what the next day could bring. Each new day is a blessing and even when it seems hopeless there is always the possibility that something can change, that something new could take place and life can be different.

I found that there were two bible verses that helped me each day when I felt like maybe I didn't want to face the day or carry on: The first one was; *"This is the day which the Lord hath made; we will rejoice and be glad in it." (Psalm 118:24 KJV).* This verse reminded me that every day was God given and that I could look at the blessings that were ahead, even when it looked bleak if you look hard enough you can find something to rejoice about. The second was; *"His mercies are new every morning, great is his faithfulness" (Adapted from Lamentations 2:22-23NIV).* This was a verse that helped me remember that whatever had happened the day before this was another day and it was a fresh start; God had given me his mercy and he was faithfully with me!

We can be tempted to think that God is all powerful and sit's up in heaven looking down on us. How does he understand my problem? Can he identify with what I am going through? Well, yes, he can! Jesus was God made flesh, Immanuel which means God with us. The reality of our God is that he lived in flesh and blood, he understands the range of human emotion from deep loneliness to great joy. He knows what it is to feel tired or to get hungry. Most of all he understands what it is to go through being abandoned, betrayed and ultimately facing terrible pain and death. I think we understand most how this was for Jesus when we look at his prayer in the Garden of Gethsemane. We read that he was in such anguish that he sweat drops of blood: he knew what he had to face and in humanity asks if he can be spared the suffering. Here is a little of the scene that took place; *Jesus went out as usual to the Mount of Olives, and his disciples followed him. On reaching the place, he said to them, "Pray that you will not fall into temptation." He withdrew about a stone's throw beyond them, knelt down and prayed, "Father, if you are willing, take this cup from me; yet not my will, but yours be done." An angel from heaven appeared to him and strengthened him. And being in anguish, he prayed more earnestly, and his sweat was like drops of blood falling to the ground. When he rose from prayer and went back to the disciples, he found them asleep, exhausted from sorrow. "Why are you sleeping?" he asked them. "Get up and pray so that you will not fall into temptation." (Luke 22:39 -46 NIV).* We see here that Jesus understands what it is to face suffering, how it is to be abandoned he can identify with our pain because he has been through it. In fact, as Jesus died on the cross and cried out *"My God, My God why have you forsaken me?"* Jesus experienced a separation from God which we won't ever have to experience. For as sin and evil were punished in his being God turned away and as he turned away it meant that he never has to turn away from you. God will never abandon you; we always have the freedom to walk away from Him, but should we choose to run to Him, his arms are now open.

It is tragic that some of us have been abandoned by the very people who should have given us the sense of love and security we needed as we grew up. The reality is that many have been abandoned: by Mum, or Dad, or sometimes both. This really was never God's best for anyone and if you are in that situation you may question why God could allow that or leave you in that position. It can leave a sense of loss that is hard to repair and defences are built to keep people out which are like brick walls. There is hope though and it says in Psalm 27:10 *"Though my father and mother forsake me, the Lord will receive me." (NIV)* God is a loving Father, in fact the Bible uses the word Abba which is more like Dad, and he wants to be there for us always. Sadly, some circumstances in life can leave people feeling like "Dad's" are anything but good but we can't look on God that way, he is full of love and compassion. Your heavenly Dad is willing and able to fill the gaps that have been there because of loss or failure of our human family. Ask Him and he will start a work of healing and you will begin to know that you need never feel alone again.

I used to feel alone quite often and the sense of loneliness we feel can be crushing. I remember well a few years back needing to get away and I went to an Island in Guanabarra Bay called Paqueta Island. It is a beautiful little Island only accessible by boat, it has no cars and the only way around is by foot or by bike. I went with a deep sense of loneliness not knowing what my future was going to look like and needing God to speak with me. It was while I was there for those couple of days that I felt God draw very close. I was able to look across at the Vista of Rio. I could look back up the bay at the mountains in the distance and one night as the sun set and the moon appeared the reflection glistened on the water and a sense of peace came over me. As I cycled around the Island and took in the views and the atmosphere, I also felt God alongside me and the word came to me; "You are not alone, I am with you enjoying this alongside you". Previously to this I had always felt I needed someone with me to share experiences like this, but it was through this I realised that my happiness is up to me. No one else needs to validate us and we can be happy just knowing we are loved and that we have a maker who is happy in the creation he made us to be!

Times of being alone will come but we don't have to be lonely. We have a maker who knows our name and knows every detail of our being. He wants to be in relationship with us and is always ready to hear our cries. Know that you need never be alone, and he really will never forsake or leave you.

Application

As a bible teacher at school now I am so often asking students what application they can find from the reading they are looking at. I plan to finish each chapter with some helpful application in order to respond to the issue at which we have looked.

Firstly – If you are reading this and have not decided yet to have a relationship with God then that is the first step. We can have a relationship with our creator because of Jesus. There is an appendix at the end and it has prayer that can help you begin that relationship.

Remember this is not about joining a religion but about being part of a relationship for which you were always meant.

Meditate – Use the verses I stated in the chapter, and others, that remind you that you are not alone -

"I will never leave you nor forsake you." (Joshua 1:5, Hebrews 13:5 NIV)

"This is the day which the Lord hath made; we will rejoice and be glad in it." (Psalm 118:24 KJV)

"His mercies are new every morning, great is his faithfulness" (Adapted from Lamentations 2:22-23NIV)

Make Contact – Do not suffer in silence or struggle through things alone. I don't suggest going and blurting out your issues to a stranger but find someone you can trust to whom you can talk.

Being part of a Church can be helpful as it is a place you should be able to share with other people who will care for and help you. Sometimes this is not the case but ask God to guide you to a place where he will be able to provide a supportive environment for you.

As I have passed through difficulties being part of a local church has always been such a help to me: to have a Christian family with which you can connect. Even if you can't tell people what is happening sometimes just a hug or and encouraging word can be just what is needed to lift your spirit.

In the longer term have 2 or three trusted people you know you can be honest with: people you trust and who can trust you. I have an older friend who has been like a mentor and because of his experience he has been a very good support. I have others who are similar in age and we can walk together and discuss the challenges of life. A reminder from the Bible:

Two are better than one, because they have a good return for their labour: If either of them falls down, one can help the other up. (Ecclesiastes 4:9-10 NIV).

We do better with others to help us. I suggest that if you are married you also need these kinds of relationships outside of your marriage. I think that there is also strength in sharing with people of the same gender.

YOU HAVE AN ENEMY!

I don't know if you've read the "Lord of the rings", or watched the film? There is a scene in which Gandalf goes to visit Theoden king of Rohan. Theoden has turned pale, old and frail and is no longer leading his people. He has an advisor who continually whispers in his ear called worm tongue. Worm tongue has kept the King oppressed with lies for many years and he really controls things. Gandalf enters the scene and rebukes worm tongue with these words: "Be silent, keep your forked tongue behind your teeth. I have not passed through fire and death to merely trade words with a witless worm". He then proceeds to release Theoden from all the lies that have been fed to him over the years. Theoden suddenly changes from an oppressed weak old man back into the strong King he was always meant to be. This is a good picture of how our enemy, Satan, would like to keep us; oppressed, weak and frail, stuck listening to all the lies and unable to be all we were meant to be. We have one, Jesus, who passed through death and hell to free us from the lies that would oppress us.

Jesus said this about the enemy *"The thief comes only to steal and kill and destroy; I have come that they may have life, and have it to the full." (John 10:10 NIV)* The enemy comes to rob us and lie to us about who we really are. How often do you see that on the verge of something beautiful or joyful happening in life we are robbed of the joy of that time because another bad thing happens and takes away what was going to be such a blessing! Do you think that was God? Do you think a loving Father would throw sickness on his son or daughter? Yes, we go through bad things and yes, we can learn from them but that does not mean God inflicted it on us.

He is a loving Father who wants the best for His children.

What did Jesus go on to say? That he had come so we could have life to the full! The life that was always intended for us was a blessed and good life but we live in a fallen and sinful world that often robs us of those blessings. However, Jesus came to bring redemption, to turn the bad things around for good!

We read often of situations in the Bible that come from a bad or difficult circumstance and then God uses it for good. To name some of those stories, Joseph, Moses, David in the Old Testament, Paul in the New Testament. Look at the story of Jesus the darkest and worst death anyone could face yet out of it comes the salvation of all mankind. On resurrection morning weeping is turned into Joy as creation and humanity awakens to its redemption!

We go through the darkness but at the end of it is often the Joy. *For the joy set before him he endured the cross (Hebrews 12:12 NIV)* Jesus went through the cross but the other side was the Joy of resurrection and salvation!

One of the first scriptures that God gave me, through the difficult time, was this; *"When the enemy comes in like a flood the spirit of the Lord will raise up a banner against him." (Isaiah 59:19 KJV)* This verse was a huge encouragement to me, and it will form part of the subject of this chapter and the next. For me, it really did feel like the enemy had come in like a flood to my life. What happened was a shock and suddenly I felt overwhelmed, just as you would in a flood.

You might remember in 2005 hurricane Katrina. It is thought to have been the deadliest hurricane since 1928 taking 1,836 lives. I remember watching the news unfold and how the levees in New Orleans failed which caused much of the flooding. It was a truly horrifying event and would be termed an overwhelming event. I also remember then in the months that followed seeing many reports of how organisations, churches and individuals pulled together to help one another. The enemy did come in like a flood devastating lives and communities.

However, what happened afterwards was that a standard was raised as people rallied to help one another. Often in the face of overwhelming situations we see the standard of love raised above the circumstance, and out of the pressure and pain something beautiful is birthed.

We see Jesus encountering the devil in the wilderness in Luke 4. In each encounter with Jesus, Satan always began his question with *"If you are the son of God?"* You might have heard this before, but it is worth repeating, Satan firstly questioned Jesus' identity. We find ourselves in the same circumstance often with the enemy asking us things like; "If you are a child of God why did God let your brother die?" "If you are a child of God why were you abused?" "If you are a child of God why did you do that?" and a thousand other questions!

Our identity is questioned but the Bible is clear; *See what great love the Father has lavished upon us that we should be called children of God! And that is what we are! (1 John 3:1 NIV).* You are God's son or daughter and he wants the best for us. The lies we entertain would have us believe that God is not for us. However, one day we will stand in God's presence and there fully understand His purpose through the pain. Jesus willingly came and died on the cross so we could take our place as God's children. As He is the King that makes us princes and princesses of the Kingdom, what a wonderful reality.

One of the other things that Satan tried to do in Luke 4 was to stop Jesus from fulfilling his destiny. All of the other temptations Satan used would have diverted Jesus from his ultimate mission. If he had given in to any of these temptations, he would not have reached the cross which was his ultimate purpose to save us all. Much in the same way the liar would try to divert us from the purpose for which God made us. Maybe you have something in your heart that you feel God has asked you to do. Maybe you had a clear call from God about what he wants you to do. Many things will seek to distract you from this, some of them very good, but ultimately not your purpose.

I recall well wondering if I had ever heard from God and if I had made a huge mistake. Was it all just my imagination? However, if God has said something then his purpose will stand. The only way we can lose this is if we are diverted from our purpose. There is a very good verse in *Numbers 23:19 God is not a human that he should lie, not a human being that he should change his mind. Does he speak and then not act? Does he promise and not fulfil?* This verse shows us clearly that God is faithful to do what he says he will do. It is an interesting verse and I suggest going and reading the surrounding story. There was a man called Balaam who had been asked to curse the people of God and found he could not. In Balaam's response to Balak, who had asked him to curse Israel, this verse was part of his answer. This just demonstrates how God will always keep his promise and his word!

Understand, then, you have an enemy who lies to you. These lies attack on two fronts. Firstly, to make you doubt your identity as a child of God, secondly to keep you from fulfilling the purpose for which God made you. God is on your side and his purpose for your life is good!

Application
In this battle we need to counteract the lies with truth. Sometimes it is helpful to take scripture, a little like medicine, in doses through our day. This is because it can be the lies in which we have believed are deeply buried.

You could find a key bible verse that applies to your situation and speak it out through the course of the day. Here are some suggestions –

It is often helpful to quote things out loud as they tend to stick more in our mind and in our spirit. So maybe before beginning say ..

(Insert your name here) _____ listen to this – (Now quote the following-)

I can take every thought captive and make it obedient to Christ.

(2 Corinthians 10:5)

I have the mind of Christ (1 Corinthians 2:16)

I can know God's will and have all spiritual wisdom and understanding (Colossians 1:9)

I am a child of God (1 John 3:1)

I have been crucified with Christ (Galatians 2:20)

I have been raised up with Christ and am seated with Him in the heavenly places

(Ephesians 2:6)

My life is hidden with Christ in God (Colossians 3:3)

I am holy and blameless in God's sight because I am in Christ (Ephesians 1:4)

I am a member of God's household. (Ephesians 2:19)

My body is a temple of the Holy Spirit (1 Corinthians 6:19)

I can bear fruit in every good work (Colossians 1:10)

He will work in all things for my good because I love Him and have been called according to

His purpose (Romans 8:28)

He will meet all my needs (Philippians 4:19)

You can use 2 or 3 of these or all of them. As you speak truth over your life you will find that the lies get quieter and the truth of who you are will begin to become clearer.

LOVE LIES

The film and entertainment business make much of their revenue on the love stories they sell us. If you watch many a romantic film, there is regularly a version of love that is sold. It is about finding the one true love who will fulfil you and then when you get together you will eventually live happily ever after! It is a nice fairy tale and words of Jerry Maguire, "You complete me!", are often what we believe. If we just find that special someone then we will be complete, and life will finally make sense. Sadly, many people find themselves feeling incomplete because they never met that special someone! Alternatively, a couple do get together but then find the other person, of whom they thought so much, actually takes more away from them or gives more challenges than actually bringing any completeness.

I think that we have believed lies about love and these have then left us feeling like we are unloved, or love is an unattainable goal for our lives! I want us to unpack some of these lies in this chapter and then look at what love really is.

I mentioned a Bible verse in the previous chapter and said that it would also form part of this

Chapter. The verse was *"When the enemy comes in like a flood the spirit of the Lord will raise up a banner against him." (Isaiah 59:19 KJV)*. We talked about the enemy flooding in, but now let's look at the banner that is raised. I might not be theologically correct here, but the bible talks about a banner that is raised over us *"Let him lead me to the banquet hall, and let his banner over me be love!" (Song of Songs 2:4)*. I think that we need to understand just what love is and just how we are loved. Especially through troubles or darkness it is so important to know we are loved. Our Father raises his banner of love above us when our enemy seeks to drag us low with all the lies he would seek to sow. So, as we move forward let's expose some of the incorrect understanding of love and read just what we know love to really be.

Happiness

Many believe that if they can just fall in love with the right person, they will be happy. For many people, love equals happiness. How often have you heard people say, "I just want you to be happy"? Happiness comes and goes and is really based on what we feel at the time. I don't think any of us really experience happiness all the time: life is a roller coaster and you must ride the good and the bad! You may have seen the film "The Pursuit of Happiness". In the film a Father has lost everything but continues to pursue work and his dreams and the film's title sums things up. However, if you look more closely at the film in many senses it's about a Father who loves his son and is willing to go through a lot of difficulty and trials so that his son will be safe. Though it is about pursuing happiness, really much hardship and pain are faced to get to where he needs to for his son. Love is far more than just being happy!

Selfishness

Much self-help advice and many counsellors teach about learning to love ourselves. This is very true. We will not love others much if we don't love and appreciate ourselves. Jesus said, *"Love your neighbour as you love yourself"*. The reality is if we hate ourselves, we will hate others. It is important to know that we are precious to God and he fully accepts us as we are; warts and all!

Self-love is required but I want to point to when this gets out of balance. Sometimes it becomes selfish love! We have needs and those needs should be met so we find ourselves looking to meet them. This can often be at the cost of those around us and they can become collateral damage in our pursuit to know love! We need to be very careful about how our needs are met. Sometimes love means we go without, or make a sacrifice, give something up and that is not always about loving ourselves. However, in the end we might find doing the difficult thing really *was* about finding our own love too!

I was watching Gumball (A kids TV show) with my kids and there was a very funny moment where a girl was trying to convince the main characters, Gumball and Darwin, that life was not all about them. She said with an accent "It's not about you!' this was repeated by Gumball as "It's not about chew? What does she mean?". So, then she cries louder "It's not about *you*" and they still misunderstand. The girl tries one more time. They don't get it, so she walks away! The scene is quite funny, you probably need to watch it to see the humour! There is a point to me telling you this... Life is not all about you! Yes, you matter, yes, your dreams and purposes are important. But we all need to learn that we exist in community and our selfishness often separates us from the love we so desperately crave because we often make it all about ME!

Sexual pleasure

It appears to me that in the media and even on social media many things are sexualised. Now. sex, apparently, has become something that each of us should have and have enough to satisfy us. It has become a need to be satisfied equal to having a meal or a snack that will stop our stomach groaning. Our lustful desires are now just on the level of our hunger and need to be satisfied in much the same way. We would be led to believe that love is found only when this need is satisfied and this is making love?

I remember watching the series "friends" when it first came out in the nineties and in one episode Ross inappropriately kisses his very attractive cousin. It was a humorous scene. Even back then though his excuse was "I'm sorry, I haven't had sex in a very long time". As if a lack of sex leads us to do inappropriate things or that if we are not getting enough, we are somehow "strange"!

15

Since the ninety's things have gone a lot further and now that would be considered very tame. Stop for a moment though and think, am I not of value if I can't have a proper sex life? Of course not!

Now I am not a kill joy, sex is something God given and can be great fun and a blessing. It does have a purpose though. It is not just a need to be met like our hunger. From a Christian perspective it has a twofold fulfilment: one is to tie the two people together who have sex in a spiritual bond. The act of sex between man and woman tie the couple in a covenant relationship and that is a physical coming together but also a spiritual tie. There is more to this but in the scope of this book I will not explain further, neither do I intend to get into discussions about sexuality. The second reason for sex is for procreation, a new person is being formed out of this wonderful union and it is supposed to be a united and loving environment for that child to then be born. It is heart breaking, therefore, to see how we have reduced this to just another bodily function. It is not then hard to understand why the amount of pornography has increased, the sex trafficking trade continues to grow, and child abuse is on the rise. People are just fulfilling their needs.

Now I am not in the business of condemning anyone: we all make mistakes and sex has the same buzz as a drug. If we have made mistakes, God is loving and kind and there is always a way back to our loving creator. We should consider though whether sex is really what we consider love to only be about. It is a momentary pleasure that makes us feel good for a while. Like any other drug though, the buzz does wear off, and life returns to the "normal' so to speak. Do we still feel the aching loneliness afterwards if that sexual act is only in fulfilment of a need? Ultimately the drive for this comes from the fact that deep down inside all of us have a loneliness that we want to fill. For some we try to fill that loneliness with sex, for others that could be drugs, drink or even work. Ultimately love is about more than sex.

Comfort

Our society, at least in the developed world (If we should call it that?), has become comfort driven. We want the easiest way to clean our house and our clothes. We want the most comfortable couch or a bed that massages us. We want to be insulated in our homes from noise and the outside climate if that is too hot or too cold. We want our cars to be more and more filled with gadgets that make it easier to drive from a to b. We want holidays that take us to the most exotic place with the least amount of discomfort possible. Maybe we have come to the place that love is about being comfortable?

It is possible that relationships must be comfortable and then we consider ourselves to be loved. In relationship we want the other person to sooth our ego, tell us how great we are and never disturb our precious equilibrium. It is like our social media where we just love the people who give us a thumbs up and make nice comments on our photos. God forbid that anyone might dare to ask a difficult question or be challenging to us.

The reality is that relationship requires difficult questions and us being prepared to answer them. Sometimes other people will challenge us, but we don't walk away. I remember well working with people with addictions or mental health problems, trying to be loving to them was very uncomfortable. On one occasion a lady who attended our church suffered from both mental health and alcohol addiction. She came to a Saturday morning sale we were holding in the lead up to Christmas, she was shouting and swearing at me. She said a number of things about me that were difficult to hear. In the end, I had to escort her out of the door with the help of someone else who was working with us. A week or so later that had all passed and she came to church on Sunday morning, as normal, to share in worship with us, relationship continued. Was that comfortable? No. But it was right that I should continue to show love and try to keep a relationship. I probably learnt more about myself from that than she ever gained from me.

The reality

Love is most beautifully expressed when we look at the cross of Jesus. It is not a place of happiness, comfort, selfishness or bodily fulfilment. In many ways it is the opposite of all those things. Jesus said this; *"Greater love has no one than this: to lay down one's life for one's friends." (John 15:13 NIV)* He demonstrated that love was being ready to give something away selflessly.

We understand what it is to be ready to die for someone we love who has been a blessing to us. To die for a friend or be ready to give something up for our family but to die for the wrong of another person goes against everything we would naturally want to do! Jesus went to the cross to die for people who had utterly rejected Him. He went to take every sin on himself to give us freedom. It demonstrated love in a way nothing else can. For Jesus we see that love was a choice and a decision of will. He could have turned his back on us. It was not comfortable, it wasn't happy or in any way selfish. He had to choose against the odds to love us when we were at our most unlovable. You see when we look at Jesus, we understand that he was ready to look past all of the worst characteristics about each of us and see the best in us each. For us it is easy to cast off another person when we see something ugly in their character or behaviour. We find it inconvenient to continue to choose that person. Jesus made a choice to rescue us and keep loving us even if we reject him. *That* is love.

We also must understand the origin of love. *We love because he first loved us (1 John 4:19 NIV).* Love comes from God. It was His idea. He made us to love and be in relationship. We love because in the first place he loved us! I have learnt over the years that I don't really understand how to love I have very mixed motives and my love is weak at best! I have found that I need to ask God to teach me how to love.

A great illustration of learning how to love was from the life of

Peter. Peter was a man full of passion and he wanted to love Jesus and follow him. I identify with Peter, he wanted to do the right thing and was ready to act sometimes getting it wrong, like me! If we look at him, he was the one disciple that actually was prepared to get out of the boat and walk on water for a moment; so credit to him! At one point he states to Jesus *"Even if all fall away on account of you, I never will." (Matthew 26:33)* Jesus then predicts Peter's denial and sure enough, when the time comes, Peter denies Jesus 3 times and is broken and weeps afterwards. However, there is a beautiful story at the end of John's gospel when Peter is reinstated. Jesus ask's Peter three times if he loves Him. Peter responds with, *"You know that I love you".* There is an interesting point here though when we look at the Greek word for love. Jesus asks Peter the first two times do you Agape me? Agape is the purest and most holy form of love. Peter responds with you know that I philia you: this is the friendship/brotherly type of love. The final time Jesus asks using the philia word for love and Peter responds with the same. I think that Peter has realised that he can't love Jesus with the Agape kind of love. He is not able to do so because the only one who can really love in that way is Jesus, God himself. It is almost as if Peter is acknowledging that he needs help to love as he really should, as we all do!

There are many lies out there about love but hopefully we have been able to see that love is not just feelings it is also a choice, a decision of our will, even when it is inconvenient or uncomfortable. Perhaps, we can understand too, that we need God's help to love as our love is often flawed and inconsistent. Our loving Father is the creator of love and can teach us how to love because he first loved us.

Application
Maybe the first application could be a simple prayer like this – "Father I don't know how to love you or to love others please teach me how to love!" Being humble enough to admit this and see our need is a very good start and ties to the verse; *We love be-*

cause he first loved us (1 John 4:19 NIV)

A fantastic text about love is this;

Love is patient, love is kind. It does not envy, it does not boast, it is not proud. It does not dishonour others, it is not self-seeking, it is not easily angered, it keeps no record of wrongs. Love does not delight in evil but rejoices with the truth. It always protects, always trusts, always hopes, always perseveres 1 Corinthians 13:4-7

We can use this verse and take out the word love and insert our own name asking God to develop these characteristics in our lives. It will be a lifetimes work, and we won't be perfect, but as we seek to do this God will be faithful in helping shape our character to become more loving. It is also good to meditate on other texts about love from the bible here are a few final suggestions –

John 15:9-13

Matthew 22:37—39

Romans 8:39

Song of Songs 8:6-7

KEEP FORGIVING

Forgiveness is something that is taught and talked about on many occasions in the Church. It is also understood in society now how important it is to forgive. Studies have been conducted on people's health and found that those who are forgiving and not bitter are generally likely to be healthier than a bitter person. You could find several good books, teachers and information about forgiveness readily available. I hope that as I write you will find something else helpful in my words that will really encourage you to live the life of forgiveness. I think that it is a lifelong lesson and we will be learning it probably all our days on this earth. As a Pastor I had taught often about forgiveness, what it meant, our need for forgiveness, how we receive forgiveness and so on. In my ministry as a Church leader I also found that often I could become the object of peoples anger or frustration and I needed to forgive people for some harsh things that had come my way. I felt I understood forgiveness and had resolved to live my life trying to be someone who forgave. However, practical realities often test our well learned theories and I found that my theory was really put to the test! When you must action forgiveness in a big way in your life is when the rubber really hits the road. I can't talk about the issue or what took place and it would not be correct to, but it is enough to say I faced a big issue with which I had to struggle through the reality of forgiving.

We really must learn that the best life is when we are free of the weight of bitterness. Bitterness occurs when we choose not to forgive. It becomes a burden and pain in our life. It says this in the book of Hebrews; *"See to it that no one falls short of the grace of God and that no bitter root grows up to cause trouble and defile many." (Hebrews 12:15 NIV)*, it helps us understand that bitterness not only affects us but those around us as well. It states not to let bitterness take root.

I was never really interested in Gardening. My Mum was. I would occasionally be subjected to "Gardeners World' on the BBC back in the day when we only had one screen in the house. Mum would often get frustrated with a weed called Bindweed in the Garden. She would pull it up and yet it would return. You see unless you got all the root of Bindweed out it simply grew back. Bindweed is a good illustration of how our bitterness can just grow back. We must uproot it completely and the tool to do this is forgiveness. There are three main areas in which we need to practice forgiveness.

Firstly, forgiving others, secondly forgiving ourselves and finally forgiving God. You might cry, how can I forgive God? After that last one, I will come to that.

Forgiving Others

We all make mistakes and part of that is we make selfish choices on a regular basis. Sometimes today when the word sin is spoken it is seen as irrelevant to consider things as sin. Sin is very real and destructive but maybe a good way to think of it is that it comes from selfishness and really causes separation in relationship. That separation happens between people, but it also causes separation in our relationship with God. Forgiveness is part of the work of repairing broken relationship, For one who is not prepared to forgive then separation becomes a large part of life. We hurt others and others hurt us because of this selfishness or brokenness. The way to maintain relationship is to be prepared to forgive.

Forgiveness is a interesting thing: what could be an easy issue to one person might be a mountain of an issue to another. Issues of forgiveness can go from the need to forgive someone for saying something a little upsetting to someone needing to forgive a murderer. Whatever the issue is we must not trivialise the issue someone is dealing with when they are acting to forgive.

Forgiveness is a choice we must make. Initially the feelings might not follow but the more we choose to forgive then feelings will follow. When we forgive, we are not agreeing that what the other person did to us is right, but we are choosing to let go. It is like a debt that is too big to be repaid, we try and try to get our money back but, in the end, the other person just doesn't have the ability to pay. We can go on being anxious, fighting for the debt to be paid off and get more and more frustrated but in the end, you are the one with the anxiety and the frustration. To forgive means you let the other person off the hook which in turn releases you from the hold of bitterness. You don't need to carry around the frustration and anger anymore. We learn from Jesus when, as he was on the cross he said; *"Father forgive them for they don't know what they are doing"*. He released the men who put nails through his hands into his forgiveness. They could never make it right. There was no way for the soldiers to remove the scars and make it right but by forgiving, Jesus made them free. By His death Jesus released forgiveness for all our sin and so we too can forgive the offences of others.

Now you may be thinking, "what about justice?2 We all have an inbuilt sense of Justice. We tend to feel that things are unfair and sometimes we might think by forgiving there is no Justice. Well there are two things to consider: firstly, Jesus became a curse so we would not be cursed. In other words, he took all our punishment and sin on himself so we could go free. In that place Jesus met the need of justice, he bore the brunt of all humanities worst as he suffered on the cross. Secondly it says in *Romans 12:19 Do not take revenge, my dear friends, but leave room for God's wrath, for it is written: "It is mine to avenge; I will repay," says the Lord. (NIV)* We need to leave justice to God who can see the whole picture not just our limited view. If you want revenge then you will not be able to forgive, in fact you need to be able to come to the place where you can pray that the person who has hurt you could be blessed. That is hard! Jesus said we should bless our enemies; in other words, we should be able to be content to see the one who hurt us going on to do well and be happy in life. I found RT Kendal's book "Total Forgiveness" very helpful for me and I recommend reading it. A quote from this book says; "But how can I know that there is no bitterness left? I would reply: (1) when there is no desire to get even or punish, (2) when I do or say nothing that would hurt their reputation or future, and (3) when I truly wish them well in all they seek to do." This statement really challenged me and at the end to wish that people who have hurt you will do well. This is not easy, but it is important and ultimately will bring peace and freedom for you.

Forgiving yourself

I think for some forgiving yourself is harder than forgiving others depending on your character. If you are like me, you will probably immediately blame yourself if something goes wrong. I find that when a problem arises my first course of action is to be my own worst critic and assume that the fault must have been mine. Blame is a fool's game though; Adam and Eve started this game with Adam blaming Eve and then Eve blaming the snake and so we have all been looking for someone to blame ever since! I am not saying that there is no personal responsibility, but I am pointing out that if a mistake is made then often looking for the culprit can be a time waster.

We need to understand what it is to repent. If we have done something that is wrong, we need to be ready to accept our part in it. Repentance is about admitting our error and then having at minimum the desire to turn away from it. David in the Old testament is a good example of this. He had a man murdered and then committed adultery with the wife of the dead man. Eventually he faces his wrongdoing and when he does, he genuinely repents. We read his repentance in the words of Psalm 51. In verses 3 & 4 he says; *For I know my transgressions, and my sin is always before me. Against you, you only, have I sinned and done what is evil in your sight; so you are right in your verdict and justified when you judge. (Psalm 51:3- 4 NIV).* David recognises his sin and confesses it before God. In a similar way we must be ready to acknowledge when we have done wrong and confess it. David then goes on to say; *Cleanse me with hyssop, and I will be clean; wash me, and I will be whiter than snow. (Psalm 51:7 NIV)*

David is asking God to clean him from his sin, he realises he can't do it himself and needs God's work to do that. David did something unthinkable, but he repents, and we read later of David that *"He was a man after God's own heart".* We can do some terrible things but if we are ready to truly repent and seek God's cleansing then there is always a way back. The key is really knowing our need of God's grace and not being busy justifying our actions!

The good news is that because of Jesus we can be forgiven and restored into a relationship with our Father. Jesus came to give us grace: that is a free gift that we can't earn, we can merely accept it.

We all do things wrong and ultimately, we should all face punishment. But that was the reality of Jesus' work on the cross, he took our place so we can go free.

One of the most helpful verses is this; *If we confess our sins, he is faithful and just and will forgive us our sins and purify us from all unrighteousness. (1 John 1:9 NIV)* If we come to Jesus and acknowledge that we have sinned then we are given the gift of forgiveness and grace and cleaned up so we can stand before a holy God. God does not look on our sin but on the purity that Jesus gave us at the cross.

Having said all that, now to forgiving ourselves. Often, we confess our sin, ask for Jesus' grace but then walk away continuing to blame ourselves for the mistake. Perhaps the thoughts rattle around our head like: "If only I hadn't done that?'; "I should have thought about this"; "If only…." And so on. Regret starts to swamp us and no sooner have we confessed our sin than we are drowning again! We need to make a choice to accept that once it is confessed, we are forgiven. It is as if we lay down our huge sack of rubbish at the cross and say; "Jesus there it is thanks for what you've done but now I'll take it away again because I think I need to keep carrying it". That is disagreeing with what God says and what Jesus achieved. Leave the sack there! Walk away feeling light knowing that you are forgiven and free!

Forgiving God
I went through a period where I blamed God for what had occurred in my life. I had tried to follow the call of God on my life and went where I felt he had called me to go. As I had done so I then found that many things I had never envisioned happening took place and left me reeling. My thought process was "You called me here and now you have let this happen!". I went through a long season of questioning God and my own faith.

My writing this book is part of what came out of that. I also learned that God was ready and able to hear all my frustration and my doubts. I went to him and told him exactly how I felt. Sometimes I raged at him, but he was continually there. He did come back with answers and guided me through that giving me new revelation of who He really is. If we look at the book of Psalms we find many times where people are just honest before God about how they feel. Honesty before God is the beginning of our healing, there is no point hiding anything from Him. He knows already! Tell him how you feel and then see how he will be ready to respond and comfort you.

Forgiving God is probably the wrong way of putting it maybe it is better to understand that we let go of blaming God. God does not need forgiving: He is totally holy and good; *He is the Rock; his works are perfect , and all his ways are just. A faithful God who does no wrong, upright and just is He. (Deuteronomy 32:4)* We see from this that God is good and ultimately, he is just. We can't see the whole picture as He does and one day we will understand why. For now, we need to learn to be satisfied that our unknowns can be trusted to God who is the one who knows all. I believe one day we will see that God was acting for our good throughout our lives and His plan is a good one!

Application
Firstly, ask God to reveal any forgiveness issues in your life. As mentioned maybe you need to forgive yourself, others, God or have issues in all of these areas. The main thing is to start living out a life of forgiveness. It is not easy and at first it will be an act of will and maybe you will not feel like you have forgiven. As you choose to keep forgiving though, eventually feelings can follow. We also need God's help to forgive and if you ask the Holy Spirit to help, he is your counsellor and will stand with you giving you power beyond your own to do this. Forgiveness is not about feelings however and has to be a conscious choice we make.

Here is a prayer you could use when forgiving others –

I choose to forgive (Add the name of the person in this blank) for (Put the action that hurt you in this blank) . This made me feel (Express all your feelings to God here, remember He is big enough to hear your anger and pain!) . I choose to forgive and bless them. In Jesus name Amen.

This is just a model prayer you can use your own prayer the main thing is to forgive before God and release to Him your heartache.

You could use a similar form of prayer when forgiving yourself or God.

DON'T JUDGE ME

Recently my Children will use the phrase "Don't judge me for this but…." Normally this is related to something that they watch that might be considered "lame" by someone else, or music that they might have on. Such is the situation that friends tend to judge one another by the music or the show that is watched and if it does not meet requirement maybe they do not measure up?

We all make judgements often based on first impressions when we meet someone. Remember the old statement "Don't judge a book by its cover". Sadly, it is often the case that we do judge people by their appearance or the initial meeting we have with them.

Imagine you are sat in a restaurant and someone walks in smelling badly, dressed in ripped and dirty clothes and stumbling around our assumption might be that they are homeless and looking for food. However, I have met people who are in that kind of situation and they can't really be summed up from that initial contact. Everyone we meet has their own story and often we don't understand where they have come from in that story.

Obviously, there are times when we have to make judgement calls and we can't just stick a blindfold on to everything that happens around us. As we now know the camera does tell lies and we can be shown that anything is believable with the development of technology. It is now hard to know when something is real or is fabricated and so we have to be careful what we accept as truth. We do have to try to discover the difference between fact and fiction in a world where things are increasingly corrupt, and truth is something that is just considered relative.

Judgement of others, however, is dangerous ground and can be damaging for us personally and for those around us. I found that judgement was a problem in my own life and I often stood ready to be judge and jury of a situation having a deep sense of what I believed to be right. I found this came from pride that had built up over the years in what I thought was an upright life. I discovered to my cost that I was not humble enough and hadn't really understood the concept of grace.

Judgement is linked quite closely to forgiveness and when we judge people it is hard to forgive them. We talked about the need for forgiveness in the previous chapter and this is an ongoing life lesson, but I think the same is true when it comes to judgement.

Jesus stated the following - *"Do not judge, or you too will be judged. For in the same way you judge others, you will be judged, and with the measure you use, it will be measured to you. "Why do you look at the speck of sawdust in your brother's eye and pay no attention to the plank in your own eye? How can you say to your brother, 'Let me take the speck out of your eye,' when all the time there is a plank in your own eye? You hypocrite, first take the plank out of your own eye, and then you will see clearly to remove the speck from your brother's eye."* (Matthew 7:1-5NIV)

This is a very important passage and I believe it is one we should take seriously and try to grasp hold of on every level. Firstly, the second part of the passage is important as we are often more ready to look at other people's issues that look seriously at our own. The comical picture Jesus paints of us trying to take a speck out of someone else's eye when we can't see the plank we have in front of us! There is always someone else to blame, it seems to be human to apportion blame as mentioned in the last chapter. It is often someone else's fault and usually for a good reason that we can find. Perhaps if we were ready to look inwardly before looking outwardly then things would become clearer. This is not to say that we are not hurt or broken by the actions of others, but it would be a good process to look at our own heart first before we take the question to others.

The first part of Matthew 7 states that by the measure we use it is will be measured to you. Firstly, we must understand what it is to measure. It used to be the case that builders would use a plumb line to measure if a wall was straight and true. A plumb line is a piece of string with a weight at the bottom and it can be hung against a wall it becomes clear quickly if the wall doesn't measure up. We tend to do the same to other people we hang a line against them and if they don't measure up we decide that they are not fit for purpose. We can then dispose of a relationship or friendship because someone does not meet our standard or fulfil our need. However, Jesus is telling us here that the line we use against others will be the same measure for us, so if we decide that something is wrong in someone else, we need to be ready to use the same measure for ourselves.

Linking back to the earlier chapter about forgiveness Judgment can be linked to bitterness. If we allow judgement to take root it becomes a bitter root judgement against someone else. This then informs our opinion of people and we then have an expectation that they will behave in a certain way. This could be if we are failed, we judge the individual for it and then we expect that is what they will always do. Another example would be if a friend is cruel with their words and we judge them we then expect that this is how they will behave in future. In the end we start to receive these things back on ourselves the measure we use ends up being the measure we receive.

Recently we have been re-watching the Star War's prequels which chart the rise of Darth Vader. Some have said these are the worst of the Star Wars series, but I think they are quite good giving the background for the other films. Darth Vader starts as young Anakin Skywalker a young boy who along with his mother find themselves as slaves. He dreams of leaving his situation and becoming free. As the plot unfolds, he becomes a powerful Jedi being trained by Obi-Wan Kenobi. However, he gradually gets turned to the dark side and the power that was to be used for good gets used for evil. I won't go into the plot but if you watch the films you will see that much of this is down to judgements that he makes about the people around him. He then gets a warped sense of justice which eventually turns into actions that are way beyond where he started. We must be aware that often when we judge people in a wrong way it can become twisted and that what started out as a sense of injustice can go beyond this to bitterness and eventually lead us down a destructive road.

Ultimately when we become a judgemental person it separates us from other people and from God. We need to lay aside our judgement and ask God to help us see people through His eyes. Jesus was full of grace and truth; He told the truth but always with grace and love in his heart to bring growth and change in those he was around. We could all benefit from having more grace in our lives and in the world.

Application
You could use the scripture we mentioned earlier on which to meditate and maybe memorize.

"Do not judge, or you too will be judged. For in the same way you judge others, you will be judged, and with the measure you use, it will be measured to you." (Matthew 7:1 NIV)

As you do this remember that your measure for other people is the same measure you should use on yourself.

In prayer ask God if there are people in your life that you have judged too harshly. If some come to mind, ask God's forgiveness and then ask him to uproot any bitterness in you. It might be appropriate to seek someone's forgiveness, be wise in this, it is not always the case. Sometimes it is just between us and God. If we involve another person is it because they could benefit from us approaching them? It is not for our own relief!

Finally, simply pray that God helps you to have a better understanding of his grace. We have all received so much from His grace and often we do not give this kind of grace to others.

NO MORE PITY PARTIES

Have you ever heard the expression; "Let him wallow in it". This is often expressed about someone after a failure or a defeat of some kind. It is then said as a derogatory remark about their situation. It is often after some kind of disappointment that we do tend to wallow in our own self-pity. We may say things like; "Why did it happen to me?", "It's not fair". "If only I had done that differently" and many more. It becomes a self-analysis of our failure and a downward spiral of looking back at what was unjust or what we could have done differently.

The definition of self-pity is; excessive, self-absorbed unhappiness over one's own troubles. This is very helpful as it can explain how this gets us. We become self-absorbed in unhappiness; this is a place where hope gets lost. It seems to become the situation that we can no longer see the good things around us and focus inwardly on all the bad.

I had a pretty hefty dose of my own self-pity and it led me down a dark path. In the end I was wondering if my existence was even worthwhile. I was busy looking at all the things I had lost, all the things I could have achieved and all the dreams that were now lying shattered. I could no longer see what I had. A quote from Joyce Meyer helped me tremendously: she said; "Don't focus on what you have lost, inventory what you have left and start using it with a grateful heart" I started to make a conscience effort to look at the positive things for which I could be grateful and chose to stop looking at my failures or losses.

I had also known Philippians 4:4-7 for a long time, which says; *"Rejoice in the Lord always. I will say it again: Rejoice! Let your gentleness s be evident to all. The Lord is near. Do not be anxious about anything, but in every situation, by prayer and petition, with thanksgiving, present your requests to God. And the peace of God, which transcends all understanding, will guard your hearts and your minds in Christ Jesus."* I had learnt this scripture to help me with anxiety but as I looked at this, I found the practice of finding everything I could for which to thank God lifted me out of self- pity and started to restore my peace.

Self-Pity is often a response to dealing with disappointment or failure and is a response that God does not really desire for us. Really failure and disappointment can be a learning opportunity and a great place for growth and development. All too often, however, these lead to bad responses and then destructive behaviour. We can learn from two biblical characters about their responses to this. Firstly, we can look at Judas who made the wrong response to his failure. Secondly, we can observe Peter's response which leads to a much healthier and restored place for him.

Judas was a disciple of Jesus he had spent time with all the other disciples and Jesus. He had seen all the miracles, witnessed Jesus' compassion and heard all of Jesus' teaching. However, he made a decision to betray Jesus. We don't get a complete picture of why he did this. He could have been motivated by the offer of thirty pieces of silver. Another motivation may have been that he wanted to push Jesus' into showing his power and destroying the Romans. We know that Judas was a Zealot and this group longed to see the restoration of Israel and the destruction of the Roman oppressors. We don't really know what went on in Judas' heart: what we do know is where it led. Failure. Judas must have felt that his failure was so great there was no way back and we read:

"Early in the morning, all the chief priests and the elders of the people made their plans how to have Jesus executed. So they bound him, led

him away and handed him over to Pilate the governor.

When Judas, who had betrayed him, saw that Jesus was condemned, he was seized with remorse and returned the thirty pieces of silver to the chief priests and the elders. "I have sinned," he said,
"for I have betrayed innocent blood."
"What is that to us?" they replied. "That's your responsibility."

So Judas threw the money into the temple and left. Then he went away and hanged himself." (Matthew 27:1-5)

We see from this that Judas must have understood he had sinned, and it also says he was full of remorse. He regretted what he had done but shame and guilt made him turn to the only way he could see out. We could suppose that self- pity played a large part in the fact that he ended hanging himself, he maybe could not see anything good and only focused on his failure seeing no way back. The opportunity for growth or change was lost and the story ends sadly.

Now we turn to Peter. Peter was one of the three disciples who were closest to Jesus. Peter was such a significant figure in the life and stories of Jesus. He also become one of the foundational fig-ures of the early church. However, Peter had his own failures. The greatest of these failures was his denial of Jesus after His arrest. We must start at the beginning and see what took place..

"Simon, Simon, Satan has asked to sift all of you as wheat. But I have prayed for you, Simon, that your faith may not fail. And when you have turned back, strengthen your brothers."

But he replied, "Lord, I am ready to go with you to prison and to death."

Jesus answered, "I tell you, Peter, before the rooster crows today, you will deny three times that you know me." (Luke 22:31- 34)

This discussion with Peter happened at the last supper. The dis-ciples had just been discussing who would be the greatest in the Kingdom of heaven. After this Jesus turned to Peter, calling him by his original name (Simon), and said that he would be sifted by Satan. What does it mean to be sifted? We use a sieve to make something finer. Like flour we may want to remove any impurities. In this situation I think Jesus was trying to explain to Peter that there were some issues in his life that needed bringing out to make him stronger and ready for what would lie ahead for him. Jesus assured him that he had prayed for him and that his faith would not fail. Reading on we then see that Jesus predicted Peter's denial. Later we see that Peter does deny Jesus three times and afterwards when the cock crows it says he went out and "Wept Bitterly". The failure happened and obviously seeing Peter's response we understand that he must have regretted it.

There is a difference here between Peter's response to failure and that of Judas. Peter did grieve his failure and that is normal. If you have failed, been betrayed or hurt in some way it is normal to be upset and need to express that in some way.

It states in *1 Corinthians 7:10 "Godly sorrow brings repentance that leads to salvation and leaves no regret, but worldly sorrow brings death."* So, we understand that sorrow that God intends in our lives will lead us to repent. This kind of sadness leads us to a place that means we can change for the better and ultimately be made stronger. Regret can be a destructive force and if we look back at Judas this was what led to his demise. Here we read that godly sorrow leaves no regret, if you have regrets God can take those from you when you come to a place of repentance and change. If we just wallow in worldly sorrow in the end it leads to death. Maybe we could say if we wallow in Self- Pity it will lead to death.

Now if we look back at Peter, we see that he was being sifted and the issue that was really raised in his life was pride. He was proud in who he was and maybe reliant on his own strength instead of God's. Now it is easy to point to Peter about pride, but I think this is an issue I faced and that, in reality, we all do. It is actually counter cultural to depend on God instead of being self-dependent. Society actually praises our independence and ability to stand alone. Peter had to face this issue in his life and, in the end, he would be a stronger person for going through this process.

There is a beautiful scene at the end of the book of John where Peter is restored by Jesus. We read;

When they had finished eating, Jesus said to Simon Peter, "Simon son of John, do you love me more
than these?"
"Yes, Lord," he said, "you know that I love you."
Jesus said, "Feed my lambs."
Again Jesus said, "Simon son of John, do you love me?"
He answered, "Yes, Lord, you know that I love you."
Jesus said, "Take care of my sheep."
The third time he said to him, "Simon son of John, do you love me?"
Peter was hurt because Jesus asked him the third time, "Do you love me?" He said, "Lord, you know all things; you know that I love you."
Jesus said, "Feed my sheep. Very truly I tell you, when you were younger you dressed yourself and went where you wanted; but when you are old you will stretch out your hands, and someone else will dress you and lead you where you do not want to go." Jesus said this to indicate the kind of death by which Peter would glorify God. Then he said to him, "Follow me!" (John 21:15-19 NIV)

There is an important understanding here that I think helps to explain Jesus' three questions. In English there is only one word for love but in Greek there are a number of words that can be used. Here we see the use of the words, Agape, which is the purest form of love like the love God has for us. The other word used is Philia which is the word that is used for the kind of love between friends. Initially when Jesus askes Peter if he loves him he uses the word Agape and Peter responds with Philia. This is significant as I think it shows that Peter is no longer full of pride but has realized he does not know how to love as Jesus does that his love can only be that of a friend. Peter has been through sorrow and come to realize his need of God, pure love can only come from God. We can learn from Peter that failure is not the end but can be a great opportunity for change and growth. He goes on to become such a significant influence in all that followed after Jesus returned to Heaven and the Church began.

Have you failed or experienced a loss or betrayal of some kind? Don't wallow in it. Look for what you can learn from it and how you can move forward. Ask God to help you through and bring about the place of freedom from your regrets.

When we look at Peter's restoration there are some other beautiful details that are here. Peter is fishing and Jesus arrives on the shore, it was a reminder of the first call of Peter. It must have come back to Peter's mind. The large catch of fish must have reminded Peter of the time Jesus had done this before.

Finally, the three questions Jesus asked were difficult, but we can almost see how they take back the three denials and drive away his regret. Jesus can lift you from your self- pity and bring restoration!

There was a day in Rio when I was wondering how the future would turn out and what I would do next. I was struggling with my own loss and self- pity. That morning I was making pancakes for my children and as I watched one bake in the pan a beautiful heart shape appeared on the pancake. For me this was God saying it's ok I love you. I called Deborah and Zech and showed them. It was an encouraging moment for us all. Then at the end of that same day we had been for a lovely walk in a nearby forest when we returned home there was a storm and as we looked out from our balcony a beautiful double rainbow appeared over the hills in the distance. I always remember God's covenant promise whenever I see the rainbow. For me it was another affirmation of His presence with us. God can lift you out of your darkest moments and he will use details that are specific to you. Allow him to help you and watch how he can bring restoration to you even in the detail of your life!

Application
Tell God all about the things you have lost and the pain you feel. He is ready to hear! Cry, shout and scream. Once you have done this make a decision to stop looking back at what you have lost.

Then begin to list all the good things you are blessed with, no matter how small. Thank God for these things and use what you have left. You could write things down each day or simply speak them out in prayer. The habit of being thankful will help to lift you from self-pity.

You could meditate or learn this verse –
"Rejoice in the Lord always. I will say it again: Rejoice! Let your gentleness be evident to all. The Lord is near. Do not be anxious about anything, but in every situation, by prayer and petition, with thanksgiving, present your requests to God. And the peace of God, which transcends all understanding, will guard your hearts and your minds in Christ Jesus." Philippians 4:4-7

Find someone else to help with their problem! I know that your situation is hard, and you could really do with the help right now! However, if you seek to help someone else it will shift your focus and help you to realize that you are not alone.

NO ROOM FOR PRIDE

I had a big lesson to learn about pride, I was a man who thought he was humble; in itself that is a problem! Life had treated me pretty well; I had followed the calling of God on my life. I met a beautiful lady who I married, and we had two amazing children. We shared common beliefs and vision and worked together in ministry. We both were called to Brazil and had waited for years to actually find ourselves being sent to Rio de Janeiro.

I remember a few months before leaving for Brazil saying to my then wife; "I really don't think I have any regrets in life". I recall her looking at me strangely as if to say; "are you sure about that?" What a prideful man I was and unaware of many of my shortcomings and little did I know what regrets I would have to face. I had to face my own pride in the end and God allowed me to face some serious humbling! I needed to see that I really had not done so well on my own. Though I was a Christian and a Pastor, though I loved God, I was still full of self and pride.

In the last chapter we looked at Peter and how he had to face failure but part of that was seeing his own pride. He was ready to die for Jesus, or so he thought: when the time came though he denied Him. He went through a failure which humbled him but then brought him to a new place of dependence on God. When I look back now it was a similar situation for me: I had to take a long hard look in the mirror and realize that I wasn't as passionate, obedient and spirit led as I may have thought!

Pride is really when we look at our own achievements and get a sense of satisfaction out of them. This is not always a bad thing, but it can become a god to which we bow down, We can become like a little child in front of a parent saying; "God look at what I have done.   Aren't you pleased with me?" Ultimately, I had to come to the place where I understood that before God all of my achievements don't amount to much. He made me, he knows everything I have to offer and all I do already. Who am I before Him? All I can really offer is my sincere thanks and my love.

Proverbs 16:18 says; *"Pride goes before destruction, a haughty spirit before a fall."* Pride can ultimately lift us up and we think that we are standing on something good that we have built all in our own strength. Eventually the platform we are stood on comes tumbling down like a house of cards and we find ourselves on the floor wondering what just happened. It is in this place though that we can encounter God in a new way and out of this our dependency can shift from self to Him.

Job is a good story to look at and is often referred to when we are dealing with the issue of suffering. We can also find in this story a lesson about dealing with pride and in the end how Job saw that before God his achievements were nothing of which to be proud! Job was considered a good man: he had obeyed God, he had been righteous and had cared for those in need. He was a man respected by everyone around him. He found himself losing everything and then questioned himself and God.

There are three friends who come to Job and seek to reason and council him, but their council is not at all helpful. How often do we get advice from people who really don't understand or empathize with the situation in which we find ourselves? Be wise to those to whom you go when you are in distress!

In the end God spoke to Job and asked if he really knew all that God's knows. How is He able to question God as a man who only sees a part of the picture? It is interesting to read what God has to say from Job 38 - 41 he gives an understanding of just how wise and all knowing He is.

We like to think we are in control of our destiny and our lives, playing God. It is also interesting to note that God rebuked Job's friends for their foolish council. Maybe if we were able to listen to God more than other people, we might find things go better for us.

In the end we read that Job said;

"I know that you can do all things: no purpose of yours can be thwarted.

You asked; "Who is this that obscures my plans without knowledge?" Surely I spoke of things I did not understand, things too wonderful for me to know.

"You said; "Listen now, and I will speak; I will question you, and you shall answer me.

My ears had heard of you but now my eyes have seen you. Therefore I despise myself and repent in dust and ashes." (Job 42:1- 6)

Job realized that without God he is nothing, that all his achievements, possessions and work didn't amount to much without God's sustaining and protection. This is a man who had been thoroughly humbled and out of this gained a greater understanding of who God is and his need for Him. As we read on to the end of the book of Job we see that God restored Job and blessed His life. This is an encouragement that often after a period of humbling God is able to restore us.

It is important to understand that we are given this life; our relationships, our abilities and all our possessions. It is given for a period of time and eventually this life will pass away. I believe that our ability to steward who we are and what we have is really what matters. Hold lightly on to what you believe to be yours but hold tightly to God and His calling on your life! When we find ourselves in a difficult place where it seems everything is falling apart it is normal to question God. He is big enough to receive our questions, doubts and fears and I recommend crying them all out to Him. Once we have laid those questions before God though be ready to hear the voice of the Holy Spirit and accept some difficult answers but also His loving embrace.

A verse that I have found helpful is James 4:10: *Humble yourselves before the Lord, and he will lift you up.* If we bow down before God through our difficulties and acknowledge that we need him, in the end he will lift us up. God is a loving and gentle Father: he does not punish us but he disciplines us that we might grow and develop.

Proverbs 3:12 states; *"because the LORD disciplines those he loves, as a father the son he delights in."* He wants us to be the person he always made us to be, having the character that is redeemed and shining for His glory with the love of God. He also desires that we use all the gift he put within us to the best of our ability. What a great heavenly Dad we have! Trust that he is always working towards our best even through the pain and difficulties.

Application
Search your heart and see if there is any pride that is wrong. Now I am not saying you can't be proud of anything; we need encouragement and it is good to be built up: for instance, I am proud of my Children and that is right and there is no problem in that.

You could use these verses in your prayer –

Search me, God, and know my heart; test me and know my anxious thoughts. see if there is any offensive way in me, and lead me in the way everlasting. (Psalm 139:23-24 NIV)

Open your heart to God and allow him to show you the areas where you have built false pride and raised yourself up beyond God.

Try to practice dependence on God instead of self-reliance. Finance can be a good test of this, when things are tough are you willing to trust his provision?

Are there areas in your life you have closed to God, do you need to open those areas up to Him?

Go and serve others! If you don't have a place where you can offer service to someone else go and do so; Volunteer for an organisation; help a friend in need; or help a family member who needs it.

Jesus was ready to serve others in humility. He demonstrated this when he washed his disciples' feet. Service helps us to keep humble.

WATCH YOUR THINKING!

I don't know about you, but I am someone who tends to over think things and I often end up creating a scenario in my head that stops me from doing something. For instance, if I wanted to try surfing here in Rio initially, I might think that is a great idea and then I start to think on it: Well what if the instructor just wants to take my money; If the waves are too big then I might drown; I could get attacked by some shark; Then, before you know it my scenario has become some gangster taking my money (Who pretended to be a surf instructor); me getting overwhelmed by waves that are too big and then being eaten by a shark! Unlikely! I had to learn a big lesson that I needed to choose what I thought about and what I allowed to continue running around in my head.

If you don't know part of a situation or a story then the tendency is to fill in the gaps: that is something we should try not to do. We don't really know the full picture and can only deal in the facts that we do know. The danger with this is it can become a Paranoia and we believe things that are happening that are not. This can lead us to fight shadows that were never there in the first place. Thinking is important because what we think on can become a core belief about ourselves or others. Paul stated the following; *"For though we live in the world, we do not wage war as the world does. The weapons we fight with are not the weapons of the world. On the contrary, they have divine power to demolish strongholds. We demolish arguments and every pretension that sets itself up against the knowledge of God, and we take captive every thought to make it obedient to Christ". (2 Corinthians 10:3- 5NIV)*

We are in a battle and often the fight takes place in our mindwith destructive thought patterns and habitual bad thinking. If we have thought in a wrong way for long enough it can become like a stronghold in our mind. To clarify this a stronghold is a place that is built up in a battle to fortify and secure a position. From a stronghold it is possible to hold ground more easily so any enemy can't take it back without more effort. This is what Paul starts to point out here: that if a bad thought pattern takes hold it can then become a strong position that is hard to tear down. For instance, you might have failed at learning to swim as you grew up; you then believed that swimming is unachievable for you;, you then start to think about the failure in this; perhaps someone told you that you will never swim. In your mind this could then become a stronghold of thinking: I can't swim; I will never swim; it is too hard; I am a failure at this. This then prevents you from ever trying again! Of course, you could try again and there is a very good chance that you would be able to learn to swim, you may even find that you are good at it! This is a simple example but there can be far more sinister things that can take hold in our minds and we need to ask God to reveal these and help us to dismantle the wrong thinking we might have.

As we read on in these verses from 2 Corinthians, we see that Paul says we take Captive our thoughts and make them obedient to Christ. Do you think every thought that enters your head is just yours and so there is nothing you can do with it? That is not the case. At the beginning of this scripture we understand that we are fighting a battle. It is the same with our thoughts. Thoughts can come from our own fallen nature, in Christian speak this is often called the flesh. We are not as we were meant to be and part of God's rescue plan through Jesus was to bring restoration to our broken human nature. Thinking can be broken in this way just because we are not perfect and as such our thinking is also corrupted. It can also be the case that the enemy can place thoughts in our head. This is the Spiritual battle we fight that Paul eludes to here. In this regard thoughts might be: "I am a failure"; "I will never achieve anything"; "Everybody hates me". A loving God who has a heart to Father us would not place that in our mind so where do these thoughts come from? They are part of the battle we have to engage in and so when they enter our head we must take them Captive and Submit them to the truth in Jesus.

I often say to my children that what enters through our eyes or ears stays in our mind. It is important that we filter what we are prepared to allow into our minds. I am amazed at the progression of darkness in our world. I was watching the latest Star Wars film at the Cinema with my kids and beforehand two adverts came on for other films. As I sat and watched I was upset by how dark these films seemed to be and that my children were exposed to these ads. I question where the creativity comes from that we are being entertained by darkness and danger that goes beyond what was once considered too far! We should try to live in the light and part of that is to be aware of what we are watching and listening. A good measure for this comes from Philippians 4:8 which says; " *Finally, brothers and sisters, whatever is true, whatever is noble, whatever is right, whatever is pure, whatever is lovely, whatever is admirable—if anything is excellent or praiseworthy—think about such things.*" Perhaps if something does not fall into these categories, we should not be allowing it through the gates of our ears or eyes to enter our minds: it is worth considering.

The final thought on our thinking goes to Romans 12:2; *"Do not conform to the pattern of this world, but be transformed by the renewing of your mind. Then you will be able to test and approve what God's will is—his good, pleasing and perfect will."* As we have already seen we need to identify wrong patterns of thinking and be ready to take our thoughts captive, but this should lead somewhere. Ultimately, we are aiming for a mind that is transformed and working towards how God intended it to be originally. We need to put in some work, but we also need to cooperate with The Holy Spirit, you will not manage this by your own strength! If we ask The Holy Spirit to renew our minds he will start working on that: he will never force His way but he will gently point out things that need to change. You might find a stronghold that is revealed to you and need to start working on tearing it down and thinking in a new way. It maybe that there are some thoughts you need to stop in their tracks or perhaps there are things you let in your head to which you need to stop watching or listening. Whatever it might be. allow God to work in you and you will start to see your mind renewed and moving from the negativity that can be so destructive to the positive life- giving thoughts that come from The Holy Spirit living in you.

Application

Start by using the scriptures we mentioned previously as prayers

- Please transform me by the renewing of my mind!

- Help me to take captive every thought and make it obedient to you God!

Praying from scripture can be a powerful act as it is God's inspired word and it is often a starting point to reveal more.

Identify any strongholds of thinking in your mind: Are there things you have believed all your life that do not line up with the truth of God's word. If that is the case, then ask God to help you tear down the stronghold and build new patterns of thinking. It can be helpful to talk this through with someone because often we do not see our own false thinking but someone else might give a better perspective. (As always be wise who you speak to, a pastor, counsellor or trusted friend)

Finally, what are you thinking about? Use the scripture mentioned earlier to measure what you are allowing into you mind. If there are things that are destructive it might be time to stop watching or listening to them. *Finally, brothers and sisters, whatever is true, whatever is noble, whatever is right, whatever is pure, whatever is lovely, whatever is admirable—if anything g is excellent or praiseworthy—think about such things (Philippians 4:8)*

WAIT!

How are you at waiting? I am very bad at waiting and I think if we are honest, we don't really like to wait for things. Today we are also very used to the instant: watch a film at the touch of a button; speak to a friend instantly the other side of the world; order clothes online and have them delivered the next day. We like instant gratification and the world can give us this if we have the money and resources.

When we first came to Rio de Janeiro I had to learn to wait. We spent a long time at The Federal Police waiting for our Visas: I mean *hours* on end. Supermarket queues in the area we lived seemed endless and no one was in a rush: it felt like I needed to allow 40 minutes at the end of shopping to get through the check out. Finally, the bank was always busy and to pay money in, you had to pencil in a whole morning for it. People who are locals in Rio are called Cariocas and looking back now I needed to learn lessons from my friends here. They are relaxed about waiting (except when driving) they are laid back and: "well if we have to wait then there is not much we can do so chill out!"

In our walk with God waiting is vital and it was a lesson I had to learn! Often when God gives us a vision or a dream there is then a period of time we have to wait before it comes to pass. We also sometimes need to wait in the face of what might seem unjust or when we go through a period of suffering.

Waiting Through Injustice

Sometimes, when waiting through injustice or suffering, the first thing we want to do is cry out or hit back at what is wrong and this is natural. Don't get me wrong, it is not right to just sit by while injustice carries on. We do have to act. However. I learned that my initial reactions are often as bad as the injustice that I might feel has been done to me. If we lash out in reaction it can be damaging and just add to what was already a wrong situation.

There is an interesting story about Moses when he was facing the Egyptians after the Israelites had been freed: Pharaoh changed his mind and decided to take his army and chase after the Israelites. Moses found himself caught between the sea and a ferocious army who wanted revenge. What should he do? ... Stand still? What? This is exactly what Moses told the people who were complaining and fearful and were wondering why they had left Egypt. Moses answered the people: *"Do not be afraid. Stand firm and you will see the deliverance the LORD will bring you today. The Egyptians you see today you will never see again. The LORD will fight for you; you need only to be still." (Exodus 14:13- 14NIV)* This seems foolish when the odds are against you and there is no way out: but sure enough, God does deliver the Israelites. Miraculously, by opening the sea and letting them walk through. When faced with a disaster and looking for a way out we often find ourselves panicking: What do I do?; Where can I turn?; How will I get out of this? We sometimes need to hear the same thing Moses said to the Israelites; "You only need to be still". Being still in the face of adversity does not come naturally: we want to act; to be useful. Inactivity makes us feel helpless. The reality is that often in panic we react badly, and response can be destructive in this situation. Decisions made can also be poor when we are under pressure and not thinking clearly. Stopping and being still, giving the situation to God and waiting to hear his voice stops us from blundering forward and making things worse than they were before.

I remember well in our first Church we had a problem that seemed like it needed fixing and quickly. I went to university and studied Chemistry as my first studies after school, and as a scientist part of my thinking was to analyse the problem and find a solution. I used this thinking, found a solution, and thought I had done pretty well. Things moved on and as time unfolded, I realized that the solution I had found was not a good one at all. One evening a lady was at the Church and had a word from God for me. She simply asked: "Did you ask God about that decision?" I had to honestly say that I had not. I had simply found the quickest solution in my own thinking. This word changed my thinking. It was a revelation for me, and since then before making big decisions I try to wait and ask God what his word is on it. I have sometimes got these right other times been wrong but waiting and trying to discern the will of God before jumping into what we think is best is a sound idea!

There are so many verses in the Bible that are helpful when it comes to waiting. Here are three:

Be still before the LORD and wait patiently for him (Psalm 37:7 NIV)

Be still, and know that I am God; I will be exalted among the nations, I will be exalted in the earth." (Psalm 46:10 NIV)

And so, after waiting patiently, Abraham received what was promised. (Hebrews 6:15 NIV)

All of these were very significant to me through a period of waiting where I felt I needed to do something in a situation in which I found myself. The situation felt unjust and it seemed to be that there needed to be action! On a number of occasions I was at the point of doing something when I was praying about it and just at the moment I was about to act I would get a verse similar to the one above, or a message from a friend about waiting or a song would come on about God's timing or something similar. When it came to an end, I was so glad that I had waited and listened to God's counsel as I had misjudged the situation and God's solution was far better than one I might have found.

We need to assess the battles we find ourselves in, as mentioned earlier in the book: we do have an enemy. If we learn to listen to God and act when he says and be still when he says then, as he did for Moses, God will fight for us! When we face what we believe to be injustice it is good to look at Jesus' response in the face of His accusers. We read the following; *The chief priests and the whole Sanhedrin were looking for false evidence against Jesus so that they could put him to death. But they did not find any, though many false witnesses came forward. Finally two came forward and declared: "This fellow said, 'I am able to destroy the temple of God and rebuild it in three days.'" Then the high priest stood up and said to Jesus: "Are you not going to answer? What is this testimony that these men are bringing against you?" But Jesus remained silent. (Matthew 26:59-63NIV)* Jesus remained silent. Why? It was a fulfilment of prophecy but also it was perhaps because he knew the hearts of his accusers. They did not really want an answer they just wanted to hold him to the plan they had already made against him. We don't know, as Jesus did, the hearts of the people that might be accusing us or doing something wrong. Sometimes the best approach is to be silent as Jesus was because our words can just make the situation more volatile. God is a just God and we need to be ready to wait for Him to work His justice at the appropriate time.

Waiting for the promise

God will often call us, give us a dream or a vision and then there is a period of waiting. Sometimes this can seem long and we start to wonder: did God really say this?; am I just making things up?

We can look at so many people in the Bible who God spoke to and called them for a purpose. However, for many years there was then a period of waiting before that happened or maybe it didn't happen in their lifetime: Joseph waited many years until he came to the place that God had shown him as a ruler in Egypt; Moses was working in a field with sheep far from where he thought he would be until God turned up in a burning bush; David had been anointed as King but had to put up with Saul trying to kill him and eventually Saul's death before he got there. There is often a period of waiting while God teaches and prepares us for the dream He has put within us.

Many years ago, I remember going through a difficult time in ministry and in life. It felt like waiting had been going on for a long time. There seemed to be little or no fruit and what I was doing felt routine. Sure, I was trying to do what God asked and I was in the place I felt he wanted me but I was coming to the point of wanting to quit. At this point we went to a Christian conference and I remember hearing a preacher talk on this; *You need to persevere so that when you have done the will of God, you will receive what he has promised. (Hebrews 10:36 NIV)* He talked about the fact that often we are just about to receive our promise or a dream and then we give up. I don't remember much more but this verse has stayed with me and at the time it encouraged me to persevere. Many occasions since then this has come back to me when the wait seems long or the promise is delayed. I wonder how many of us miss out on what God had for us because, just before the fulfilment of the promise, we gave up or turned back instead of persevering.

Learning to wait is such an important part of our Christian walk. It is good to learn that instead of jumping ahead into things, we need to be still and hear the voice of God. We need to be able to wait when the promise seems to be delayed, or life seems to be routine. We must trust that God will bring about His purpose when he knows it is right.

Application

Go and find a quiet place where you can be alone and simply tune out of all the noise. Switch off the phone, disconnect the Wi-Fi, turn off the music and allow yourself to" be". Wait in that place and try to tune out the distractions that enter your mind. If you are like me this will seem weird at first but persevere. In prayer you could ask the Holy Spirit to simply speak to you. I find the prayer that Samuel said a helpful one and simply say *"Speak Lord, your servant is listening".*

You can also meditate on the scriptures I mentioned earlier in the chapter about waiting.

Alternatively type in "wait" on your Bible app and you will find many verses at which to look.

A further step could be to go on a retreat. There are some good Christian retreat centres. Going away to a different place gives a change of perspective. It also removes you from the circumstances that might be a struggle for you. I have found this very helpful over the years to regain focus and find the presence of God again.

Lastly, if there is a dream, vision or call in your life and the wait seems long, don't give up!

HOLD ON TO THE DREAM!

Imagine if Martin Luther King in his speech had said "I have a dream, but I am too scared to share it." Or, "I have a dream, it's too difficult to achieve." Or maybe "I have a dream, but I have given up on it." It would not have become the iconic speech we all know and maybe his influence would never have been on the level it was. The reality was that he was a man who followed his dream and never gave up on it!

I hope that this book has given you some help in facing the difficulties that might hit you and knock you reeling and off course. I believe that some of the chapters in this book are keys that can help you hold on to your dream when it seems that it might be impossible. I remember a good friend many years ago giving me a word that she felt was from God it was simple, and yet profound, "Never, never give up!" Then, I did not know what might lay ahead, but it has proved to be such a good word for me and a reminder to keep pressing into God and on with His purpose for my life.

I remember being called to full-time ministry many years ago, it was clear and from God. I then remember a few years later being called to Rio de Janeiro, this was also clear. Since then I have doubted both of these callings and thought; "Did God really say this?". It is ok to have doubts in yourself and in what you are doing but go to God with those doubts. He will remind you of the calling, vision, or dream He first places in your heart. It is the calling of God on my life that has kept me some days when everything else around seems to be going crazy. I have found it helpful to go back to the time when I know God spoke and gave me a specific direction for my life and I don't believe that changes. There is a little verse that says, *"for God's gifts and his call are irrevocable." (Romans 11:29 NIV)* For me, this says that God will not remove what he has gifted you with or take away the purpose he has for your life. We can run away, we can avoid it, but in the end, it is intrinsic to who we are and what we were made for!

The wait to come to Brazil was a very long and difficult wait! It was for me in the end 15 years from the time I heard God first speak to me about Brazil until we finally came. Being part of an international organization meant several different leaders had to make decisions about whether we could go or not. During the process, we had times when we were encouraged to learn Portuguese, and then we were told that leaders would think about us going. There were different goals we were given and the different answers we were told about the reasons for us not going or the reasons we were still needed in Britain. I remember on one occasion being told that we might as well give up on the idea as the chances of us going to Brazil were very unlikely. Then one day out of the blue we had a phone call from our line manager at the time who said, "Would there be any reason you could not go to Brazil". Things were happening in life at the time and we needed a moment to pray and think. I remember vividly being on the phone to one of my closest friends and he said to me "Well it's a no Brainer really", he was right and sure enough we accepted the offer. There is another story to this as there was another battle that followed with varying issues and our visa processes but in the end, we arrived. Little did I understand the cost of following this call, maybe if I had I would have refused there and then. However, I still believe this was the call of God and there was a purpose in us coming here to Rio de Janeiro and still believe it is where God wants me at this time.

If we look back in the book of Genesis at the story of Abraham, he was told some things that seemed crazy. God spoke to him and gave him a covenant promise and there were two key parts to this. Firstly, he would have the land that God was sending him to and secondly, he would have descendants as numerous as the stars. The first promise was more likely and was dependent on Abraham taking the action to go where God was sending him. The second part was harder as his wife, Sarah, was old and it seemed unlikely that she could have children. However, in the end, she does bear Abraham a child and the promise then begins to be fulfilled. I tell this story as often when I felt like I had got it wrong I was reminded of Abraham and specifically of this verse; *The Lord had said to Abram, "Go from your country, your people and your father's household to the land I will show you. (Genesis 12:1 NIV).* God had called me to go to another land and he had shown me where and this verse and Abraham's story reminded me often that God is certain in keeping His word.

When you feel like your world is caving in and the dream you had is lost allow God to remind you or speak to you about what he is doing. I had so many occasions when God would give me a verse, a scripture, a part of a book, a song, or a word from a friend that would just be what I needed to hear at that time. As I mentioned at the beginning of the book God does not lie, when he says something, he will keep his word (See Numbers 23:19). Sometimes we just need to wait and hear his voice, to be still as I mentioned in the previous chapter, and see what The Holy Spirit says.

When we read the story of Joshua, we see that he had been assigned to lead the people of Israel into the promised land. Moses had died and the time of wandering in the wilderness had finished, it was now time to go in and take possession of the land. We often think that when we enter our promised land everything will come together, when we finally get to the place we have been called or the vision is fulfilled. Look at the story of Joshua and you will understand that this is not the case. We need to remember that when Joshua headed for the promised land firstly there was a river to cross. After this they faced the city of Jericho, a huge well-defended wall stood between them and the city. We read of victories that were won in the story of Joshua, but we also read of defeat and it is interesting to note that when Joshua entered the promised land there were 39 kings who he had to defeat! If we reach the place of God's promise it does not mean the work is done, often it is the beginning of something new and new battles that will lie ahead for us. Those battles may feel long and difficult at times but be aware; fighting those battles is far better than going back to Egypt. Egypt was the place of slavery and the place of bondage; the promised land is a place of freedom and opportunity. I encourage you to keep looking forward to the promise and not look back to the place that you left behind, your blessing and future are ahead, press forward!

Jeremiah 29:11 states; *For I know the plans I have for you," declares the Lord, "plans to prosper you and not to harm you, plans to give you hope and a future.* This has been such a significant verse for me over the years reminding me that God has good plans for me. I have often shared it with others, and I know it has been a blessing on one occasion someone became a Christian because of this verse. When Jeremiah wrote this, it was not in an easy era, the people of Israel were about to be taken into exile and the nation was in disarray. Amid this God spoke these words to Jeremiah, even though things were hard God was reminding His people that he was working for them and one day His good plans would come to pass.

Finally, it is important to remember that we do have a final destination. If we see the promise, dream, or goal in this life as the final destination then we are likely to face disappointment. We must enjoy the journey but remember that there is a place in Heaven that Jesus has prepared for us. Jesus said *"Do not let your hearts be troubled. You believe in God; believe also in me. My Father's house has many rooms; if that were not so, would I have told you that I am going there to prepare a place for you? And if I go and prepare a place for you, I will come back and take you to be with me that you also may be where I am" (John 14:1-3 NIV)* He has a place ready for us and it is something more amazing than we can imagine. It is dependent on our response to Him, but if that choice is made, we can be sure of our destiny. I have talked to people who feel like eternity might be boring but for me, I imagine all the good things of this life without any of the bad, can you imagine? *"What no eye has seen, what no ear has heard, and what no human mind has conceived"— the things God has prepared for those who love him (1 Corinthians 2:9 NIV)* It is beyond our imagination to know what God has for us but we do know it will be good! We do need to live this life, we don't simply sit down and wait it out, I am not suggesting that. It is good, however, to remind ourselves that one day we will rest from the battle, and on those days when things here can be hard it is a great encouragement.

If we can live our lives in love with God, accepting Jesus and being guided by the Holy Spirit. If we can see that the difficulties, trials, and pain were for a reason. Nothing in this life is wasted and God can redeem and use all that we have been through. One day we will meet Jesus face to face and hear his beautiful voice say; *"Well done, good and faithful servant! You have been faithful with a few things; I will put you in charge of many things. Come and share your master's happiness!" (Matthew 25:21 NIV)*

APPENDIX

A prayer to enter a relationship with God -

Lord Jesus Christ

I am sorry for the things I have done wrong in my life (take a few moments to ask His forgiveness for anything particular that is on your conscience).

Please forgive me. I now turn from everything which I know is wrong.

Thank you that you died on the cross for me so that I could be forgiven and set free.

Thank you that you offer me forgiveness and the gift of your Spirit. I now receive that gift.

Please come into my life by your Holy Spirit to be with me forever.

Thank you, Lord Jesus. Amen

Lord Jesus Christ

ACKNOWLEDGEMENT

I would like to thank God for his constant love, guidance and care through my life. He is my closest friend and has always helped me through every situation I am grateful to Him for showing me the things contained in this book and his presence with me.

There are too many others who I would like to mention. If I mention some then I am sure I will miss others out. So to my family, friends and all those who have influenced my life, thank you!

Thanks also to those who have given me advice and helped me with this book. You know who you are and I am grateful.

ABOUT THE AUTHOR

Matthew Brown

Matthew is a Bible teacher at an international Christian school in Rio de Janeiro. He has experience as a pastor with The Salvation Army for 15 years working in London and then in Rio. Prior to all that he stud-  ied chemistry at Kingston University in London and graduated with a Bachelor's of Science. He worked in the chemical industry for 3 years before entering the Salvation Army Training College.
He is a Dad to two amazing children Deborah and Zech who he loves very much.
Matthew loves God and building a strong relationship with God through prayer and reading the Bible are foundational to his life. He beleives passionately that faith in Jesus is transformational and can bring change to individuals, families and communities. He longs to see "Your Kingdom come, on earth as it is in Heaven!"
In his past time Matt also enjoys music and plays the cornet. He likes to go on bike rides, walks and loves to see beautful scenary.

Printed in Poland
by Amazon Fulfillment
Poland Sp. z o.o., Wrocław